Bonsai Pot Wonders: Crafting Beautiful Homes for Tiny Trees

1. Introduction: The Art and Beauty of Bonsai Pots

In the realm of living art, where branches dance and leaves whisper, there exists a world of miniature wonder – the bonsai. These tiny trees, with roots in ancient traditions, have captivated hearts and minds for centuries. But behind each exquisite creation lies an unsung hero, a vessel that cradles and complements the bonsai's very essence – the bonsai pot.

The bonsai pot, a harmonious blend of form and function, serves as the foundation upon which these living sculptures come to life. Crafted from clay, shaped by skilled hands, and fired with passion, these pots are more than mere containers; they are an integral part of the bonsai's soul.

As you embark on this journey through "Bonsai Pot Wonders," you will delve into the fascinating world of bonsai pottery and uncover the secrets that elevate these miniature trees from simple plants to awe-inspiring works of art. Through the chapters that follow, we will explore the history, techniques, and styles that have shaped the art of bonsai pot making, and learn how these humble vessels contribute to the overall beauty and balance of these living masterpieces.

From the selection of materials to the intricacies of glazing, we will delve into the craftsmanship that goes into creating a perfect bonsai pot. As we journey around the globe, we'll discover the diverse cultural influences that have shaped bonsai pots and the artists who create them. We will learn how to pair the perfect pot with your bonsai species, and uncover the importance of display in showcasing your prized bonsai and pot.

Whether you're an aspiring bonsai enthusiast or an experienced potter, "Bonsai Pot Wonders" is a voyage of discovery that will open your eyes to the subtle artistry and unspoken poetry of bonsai pottery. As you turn each page, let the beauty of these tiny trees and their exquisite homes inspire you to craft your own living art and cultivate a deeper appreciation for the bonsai pot – the unsung hero that brings harmony and balance to the world of miniature trees.

So, take a deep breath, and let the journey begin – where roots embrace clay, and art comes alive in the world of bonsai pots.

2. The Bonsai-Pot Relationship: Understanding Proportions and Balance

In the delicate dance of bonsai, where leaves pirouette and branches bow, the relationship between tree and pot takes center stage. Just as a frame enhances a painting or a melody carries a song, the bonsai pot serves as the perfect partner to the living art it supports. It is this harmonious union of tree and pot that transforms the ordinary into the extraordinary, elevating the beauty of nature to new heights.

As we waltz through the world of bonsai pot proportions and balance, let us examine the elements that make this partnership so enchanting. Just as every dancer has their own unique rhythm, each bonsai tree is an individual, with a distinctive character and style. To bring out the best in your bonsai, it is essential to understand the subtle nuances of proportion, shape, and color that contribute to the overall aesthetic of your living masterpiece.

Begin by envisioning your bonsai tree as a dancer, poised and ready to take the stage. The pot should be the ballroom floor, providing a solid foundation that allows the tree to shine. To achieve this harmony, consider the golden rule of bonsai pot proportions – the tree's height should be roughly equivalent to the pot's width or depth. This creates a visual balance that allows the eye to appreciate both the tree and its container without distraction.

But the dance of bonsai is not merely about symmetry; it is a celebration of the tree's individuality. As such, the pot's shape should echo the tree's style and form. For example, a cascading bonsai, with its flowing branches and dramatic movement, would be well-suited to a tall, slender pot, while a stout, informal upright bonsai might find its perfect match in a round or oval container. The shape of the pot should serve to accentuate the tree's natural beauty, allowing its unique character to take center stage.

Color, too, plays a pivotal role in the bonsai-pot relationship. The hues of the pot should complement and enhance the tree's foliage, creating a visual harmony that allows both elements to shine. Earthy tones, such as browns, greens, and grays, are often favored for their ability to blend seamlessly with the natural world, while bolder colors, like blues, reds, and yellows, can create a striking contrast that adds depth and intrigue to your living art.

Texture, another integral element in the bonsai-pot partnership, can provide subtle visual interest and create a sense of unity between tree and container. A smooth, glossy pot might highlight the delicate foliage of a refined bonsai, while a rough, unglazed container could accentuate the rugged, gnarled bark of a more mature specimen. By considering texture, you can create a tactile harmony that enhances the overall experience of your bonsai.

As we continue to explore the intricate dance of the bonsai-pot relationship, remember that the beauty of this partnership lies in its subtlety and nuance. It is through the careful consideration of proportion, balance, shape, color, and texture that you can create a living work of art that transcends the sum of its parts. Like a dancer in perfect harmony with their partner, the bonsai tree and pot become one, transforming the ordinary into the extraordinary and revealing the true essence of nature's beauty.

3. Materials and Techniques: From Traditional to Modern Bonsai Pottery

In the enchanted realm of bonsai, where nature's whispers are translated into living art, the materials and techniques employed in crafting bonsai pots take center stage. From the earth's embrace, the potter's hand brings forth the clay, shaping and molding it into vessels that will cradle these miniature wonders. As we journey from the roots of tradition to the branches of modern innovation, let us explore the diverse materials and techniques that have shaped the world of bonsai pottery.

The story of bonsai pottery begins with the clay, the very essence of the earth from which these vessels are born. Rich in minerals and history, the clay used in bonsai pots can vary greatly in texture, color, and workability. Traditional bonsai pots are often crafted from earthenware or stoneware, clays prized for their strength and durability. These natural materials, fired at high temperatures, yield pots that can withstand the test of time and provide a solid foundation for the living art they support.

But the world of bonsai pottery is not bound by tradition alone. As we delve into the realm of modern techniques, we find a multitude of materials that offer new possibilities and creative freedom. Porcelain, a fine-grained, translucent clay, can produce bonsai pots of exquisite delicacy and refinement, while innovative materials, such as glass, concrete, and metal, expand the boundaries of what is possible in the realm of bonsai container design.

With our feet firmly planted in the earth and our eyes gazing toward the horizon, let us now explore the techniques that have shaped the art of bonsai pot making. Traditional methods, such as hand-building and wheel-throwing, have long been revered for their ability to imbue bonsai pots with the warmth and individuality of the potter's touch.

Hand-building techniques, such as slab construction, coil building, and pinching, allow for a direct connection between the potter's hands and the clay, resulting in pots that exude a sense of organic, natural beauty. These methods, though simple in their essence, can yield complex and intricate designs that celebrate the diversity of nature and the individuality of the bonsai tree.

Wheel-throwing, a technique steeped in tradition and skill, involves shaping the clay on a spinning wheel, using the potter's hands and tools to create symmetrical, balanced forms. This method, often associated with classic bonsai pot shapes, can produce an array of designs that range from the simple and elegant to the ornate and detailed. Wheel-thrown pots often exhibit a sense of fluidity and grace, reflecting the harmony and balance that are at the heart of the bonsai art form.

As we venture into the realm of modern techniques, we find a world of innovation and experimentation that pushes the boundaries of bonsai pottery. Slip-casting, a process that involves pouring liquid clay into a mold, can create intricate, detailed designs that would be difficult to achieve by hand. This method allows for greater precision and consistency in pot production, opening the door to new possibilities in bonsai pot design.

3D printing, an emerging technology that has revolutionized the world of design and manufacturing, offers yet another avenue for creative expression in the realm of bonsai pottery. With this technique, digital models of bonsai pots can be brought to life using a variety of materials, from ceramic to resin. This groundbreaking method allows for unparalleled customization and complexity, redefining the limits of what is possible in bonsai pot design.

As we continue to explore the vast landscape of materials and techniques that have shaped the world of bonsai pottery, let us remember that the true beauty of this art form lies in its diversity and evolution. From the roots of tradition to the branches

4. Crafting the Perfect Bonsai Pot: A Step-by-Step Guide

In the captivating world of bonsai, where whispers of nature become living art, the bonsai pot plays a crucial role in elevating the tree's beauty to new heights. With the perfect pot in hand, the miniature wonder takes on a new life, harmoniously entwined with its vessel. As we embark on this journey to craft the perfect bonsai pot, let us follow the footsteps that lead us through the art of pottery, creating a masterpiece that will cradle and complement the bonsai's essence.

Step 1: Choosing the Clay

Our journey begins with the selection of clay, the very foundation of our bonsai pot. Choose from the diverse palette of earthenware, stoneware, or porcelain, considering factors such as texture, color, and durability. The clay you select will dictate the pot's final appearance and how it harmonizes with the bonsai tree it will support.

Step 2: Preparing the Clay

Next, we prepare the clay, kneading and wedging it to remove air bubbles and create a consistent, workable texture. This process, though simple, is vital in ensuring the strength and stability of the finished pot, as well as the potter's connection with the earthy material.

Step 3: Shaping the Bonsai Pot

Now, we shape our pot, employing traditional techniques such as hand-building or wheel-throwing, or embracing modern methods like slip-casting or 3D printing. Whichever technique you choose, remember that the pot's shape should complement the bonsai tree's style and form, creating a harmonious balance that allows both elements to shine.

Step 4: Adding Details and Drainage Holes

With the basic form of the pot complete, we turn our attention to the details that will set our bonsai pot apart. Carve, sculpt, or add decorative elements that enhance the pot's character, and don't forget to create drainage holes in the bottom of the pot to ensure the health of the bonsai tree.

Step 5: Drying the Pot

Patience is key in the art of bonsai pottery, as we must now allow our creation to dry slowly and evenly to prevent cracking or warping. This process, known as the bone-dry stage, can take several days or even weeks, depending on the thickness of the pot and the humidity in the environment.

Step 6: Bisque Firing

Once our pot is thoroughly dry, it is time for the first firing, known as bisque firing. Place the pot in a kiln, gradually increasing the temperature to remove any remaining moisture and harden the clay. This process prepares the pot for glazing and helps prevent it from cracking during the final firing.

Step 7: Glazing the Pot

With our bisque-fired pot in hand, we can now explore the world of glazes and finishes. Apply the glaze to your pot, considering the desired color, texture, and finish. Keep in mind that the glaze's hues should complement the bonsai tree's foliage and enhance the pot's overall aesthetic.

Step 8: Glaze Firing

Now, we return our pot to the kiln for the final firing, known as the glaze firing. This process, which often requires higher temperatures than the bisque firing, will transform the applied glaze into a glassy, durable finish that will protect and beautify our bonsai pot for years to come.

Step 9: Admiring Your Creation

With the firing complete, our journey comes to an end, and we can now admire the fruits of our labor. Gaze upon your bonsai pot, a testament to your creativity, skill, and dedication to the art of bonsai pottery. Each curve, detail, and hue reflects the time and care invested in this handcrafted treasure, a vessel worthy of cradling nature's living art.

Step 10: Selecting the Right Bonsai Tree

The perfect bonsai pot deserves the perfect tree. Carefully choose a bonsai tree that complements your pot's shape, color, and style. Consider factors such as the tree's size, form, and growth habits to ensure a harmonious pairing that celebrates both the tree and its vessel.

Step 11: Preparing the Pot and Tree for Planting

Before uniting your bonsai tree with its new home, it is essential to prepare both the pot and tree for planting. Place a layer of mesh over the pot's drainage holes to prevent soil from escaping, and add a layer of well-draining bonsai soil mix to the pot's base. Gently remove the bonsai tree from its current container, teasing out the roots and trimming them as necessary to promote healthy growth.

Step 12: Planting the Bonsai Tree in Your Pot

With your pot and tree prepared, it is time to bring them together as one. Position the bonsai tree in the pot, taking care to arrange the roots evenly and maintain the tree's desired planting angle. Fill the pot with additional bonsai soil, ensuring the roots are completely covered and secure. To settle the soil and remove air pockets, gently tap the pot and water the tree thoroughly.

Step 13: Caring for Your Bonsai Tree and Pot

Now that your bonsai tree and pot are united, it is crucial to provide them with the proper care and attention they need to thrive. Water your bonsai regularly, ensuring the soil remains moist but not waterlogged. Provide the tree with appropriate sunlight, temperature, and humidity for its specific species, and fertilize and prune as necessary to promote healthy growth.

As you care for your bonsai tree and pot, take time to admire the harmonious balance they share. The pot, a product of your creativity and skill, enhances the tree's natural beauty, while the tree brings life and movement to the pot's earthy form. Together, they create a living work of art that celebrates the beauty of nature and the human touch.

In conclusion, the journey to craft the perfect bonsai pot is one of patience, dedication, and artistic expression. As you follow these steps, remember that it is the harmony between the tree and its pot that elevates the bonsai art form to new heights. May your bonsai pot serve as a testament to your love and appreciation for the enchanting world of bonsai, cradling and nurturing nature's whispers as they dance and sway in the gentle embrace of the earth.

5. Glazes and Finishes: Enhancing the Aesthetics of Your Bonsai Pot

In the realm of bonsai, where artistry and nature entwine, the bonsai pot stands as a testament to the harmony of earth and tree. As the sun's rays dance upon its surface, the pot's glaze and finish come to life, adding depth, texture, and color to the miniature masterpiece. As we embark on this journey into the world of glazes and finishes, let us uncover the secrets that transform simple clay into vessels of ethereal beauty, enhancing the aesthetics of our bonsai pots.

Step 1: Understanding the Role of Glazes and Finishes

As a painter's palette brings life to a canvas, so too do glazes and finishes breathe life into a bonsai pot. These magical mixtures of minerals, oxides, and glass fuse with the pot's surface during firing, creating an array of colors, textures, and finishes that can elevate a bonsai pot from the ordinary to the extraordinary. By carefully selecting and applying glazes and finishes, you can enhance your pot's aesthetic appeal, ensuring a harmonious balance between the container and the living art it supports.

Step 2: Exploring the World of Glazes

With a kaleidoscope of colors and effects at our fingertips, the world of glazes offers endless possibilities for creativity and self-expression. From earthy, matte finishes that evoke the rugged beauty of nature to glossy, vibrant hues that celebrate the energy and vitality of life, glazes can transform the humblest of clay pots into works of art.

When selecting a glaze for your bonsai pot, consider the tree's foliage, the pot's shape, and your desired aesthetic. Earthy tones such as browns, greens, and grays can create a sense of harmony and unity, while bolder colors like blues, reds, and yellows can add depth and contrast, drawing the eye to the pot and its living contents.

Step 3: Experimenting with Glaze Techniques

As we delve deeper into the world of glazes, we uncover a myriad of techniques that can be used to create unique and captivating effects. Layering glazes can produce a depth of color and texture that adds complexity to the pot's surface, while brushwork and stenciling can create intricate patterns and designs.

Don't be afraid to experiment with different glaze applications, such as dipping, pouring, or spraying, to find the method that best suits your artistic vision. Through trial and error, you can uncover new and exciting ways to bring your bonsai pot to life.

Step 4: Discovering the Beauty of Finishes

Beyond the world of glazes, finishes offer yet another avenue for creative expression. From the subtle sheen of a satin finish to the tactile allure of a crackled surface, finishes can add an extra layer of beauty and intrigue to your bonsai pot.

Explore the wide variety of finishes available, such as wax resist, decals, and gold or silver leaf, to find the perfect match for your pot and bonsai tree. Remember, the goal is to create a harmonious balance between the pot and its living companion, enhancing the overall aesthetic of your bonsai display.

Step 5: Firing Your Glazed and Finished Pot

With your glaze and finish selections made, it's time to fire your pot and witness the transformation. As the kiln's heat works its magic, the glaze and finish will meld with the pot's surface, creating a durable and beautiful coating that will protect and adorn your bonsai pot for years to come.

Step 6: Admiring Your Glazed and Finished Bonsai Pot

Once the firing is complete, take a moment to admire the fruits of your labor. The glaze and finish you've chosen have breathed new life into your bonsai pot, enhancing its aesthetic appeal and ensuring a harmonious balance with the tree it will support. Notice the way the light plays upon the pot's surface, revealing the depth, texture, and color of your glaze and finish choices.

Step 7: Pairing Your Glazed and Finished Pot with the Right Bonsai Tree

Now that your pot is a work of art, it is time to find the perfect bonsai tree to accompany it. Consider the tree's size, style, and coloration as you make your selection, ensuring that the pot's glaze and finish complement and enhance the tree's natural beauty.

Step 8: Enjoying the Art of Bonsai with Your Glazed and Finished Pot

With your bonsai pot and tree united in perfect harmony, take time to enjoy and appreciate the art of bonsai. Tend to your tree with care and attention, and allow the pot's glaze and finish to serve as a constant reminder of the creativity and dedication that have brought this living work of art to life.

In conclusion, the world of glazes and finishes offers a boundless canvas for self-expression and artistic exploration in the realm of bonsai pottery. By carefully selecting and applying these elements, you can elevate your bonsai pot's aesthetic appeal, creating a harmonious balance between the container and the tree it supports. May your journey into the world of glazes and finishes be filled with discovery, inspiration, and a deeper appreciation for the enchanting art of bonsai.

6. Hand-built vs. Wheel-thrown Pots: Exploring Different Bonsai Pot Styles

In the enchanting world of bonsai, where artistry and nature unite in a delicate dance, the bonsai pot stands as a symbol of the harmonious interplay between human creativity and the whispers of the earth. As we venture into the realms of hand-built and wheel-thrown pottery, let us delve into the unique styles, techniques, and expressions that define these two distinct approaches to bonsai pot creation.

Step 1: The Art of Hand-building

In the realm of hand-built pottery, the potter's touch is the guiding force, shaping and molding the clay into a vessel that cradles the living essence of the bonsai tree. This ancient technique, rooted in the very foundations of human civilization, offers a direct connection between the artist and the earth, allowing for the creation of pots that reflect the unique character and vision of their creator.

Hand-building techniques such as slab construction, coil building, and pinch pots provide endless possibilities for experimentation and self-expression. These methods allow for organic shapes, textures, and designs that echo the rhythms of nature, forming a harmonious balance with the bonsai tree that will call the pot home.

Step 2: The Magic of Wheel-throwing

In the world of wheel-thrown pottery, the potter's wheel is the guiding force, spinning and shaping the clay into a symphony of form and motion. This mesmerizing dance between the artist's hands and the spinning clay creates pots with an inherent sense of balance, symmetry, and fluidity, making them a popular choice for bonsai enthusiasts.

Wheel-thrown pots often feature clean lines, smooth surfaces, and an air of precision that can complement the carefully cultivated form of the bonsai tree. The skill and mastery required to create these pots lend them an air of sophistication and elegance, making them a sought-after addition to any bonsai collection.

Step 3: Comparing Hand-built and Wheel-thrown Pots

As we explore the worlds of hand-built and wheel-thrown pottery, it becomes clear that each method offers its unique charm and allure. Hand-built pots celebrate the organic, the irregular, and the human touch, while wheel-thrown pots showcase balance, symmetry, and a sense of controlled beauty.

When choosing between hand-built and wheel-thrown pots for your bonsai tree, consider the tree's style, growth habits, and overall aesthetic. A hand-built pot may provide the perfect contrast to a highly structured tree, while a wheel-thrown pot may bring a sense of harmony and balance to a more free-form bonsai.

Step 4: Embracing the Diversity of Bonsai Pot Styles

In the end, the choice between hand-built and wheel-thrown pots is a matter of personal preference and artistic vision. By embracing the diversity of styles and techniques that these methods offer, you can create a unique and captivating bonsai display that showcases the full spectrum of human creativity and the wonders of the natural world.

As you explore the different bonsai pot styles, remember that the true beauty of bonsai lies in the harmonious balance between the tree and its container. Whether hand-built or wheel-thrown, the perfect pot will not only cradle and nurture the tree but will also serve as a testament to the love and dedication that have brought this living work of art to life.

In conclusion, the art of bonsai pottery is a celebration of the diverse and captivating world of hand-built and wheel-thrown styles. By exploring these distinct techniques, you can uncover the unique charm and allure of each method and create a bonsai display that reflects the harmonious interplay between human creativity and the beauty of nature. May your journey into the world of hand-built and wheel-thrown pots be filled with discovery, inspiration, and a deeper appreciation for the enchanting art of bonsai.

Step 5: Experimenting with Different Techniques

As you embark on your journey into the realms of hand-built and wheel-thrown bonsai pots, allow yourself the freedom to experiment with different techniques and styles. The fusion of methods can result in captivating and unique pots, showcasing the rich tapestry of artistic expression within the world of bonsai pottery.

Step 6: Learning from the Masters

To truly appreciate the nuances of hand-built and wheel-thrown pots, study the works of master potters and bonsai artists from around the world. By examining their creations, you can glean insights into their techniques, styles, and philosophies, and apply these lessons to your own bonsai pot creations.

Step 7: Developing Your Unique Bonsai Pot Style

As you continue to explore the worlds of hand-built and wheel-thrown pottery, embrace the opportunity to develop your unique style. By combining techniques, experimenting with glazes and finishes, and pushing the boundaries of your artistic expression, you can create bonsai pots that are a true reflection of your vision and creativity.

Step 8: Sharing Your Bonsai Pot Creations

With your newfound appreciation for the diversity of hand-built and wheel-thrown bonsai pots, consider sharing your creations with fellow bonsai enthusiasts, friends, and family. By showcasing the fruits of your labor, you can inspire others to explore the enchanting world of bonsai pottery and contribute to the rich tapestry of styles and techniques that define this captivating art form.

In conclusion, the exploration of hand-built and wheel-thrown bonsai pots offers a journey into the heart of human creativity and the wonders of the natural world. By embracing the unique charm and allure of these distinct techniques, you can create bonsai displays that celebrate the harmonious balance between the tree and its container, and the endless possibilities that lie within the world of bonsai pottery. May your journey be filled with discovery, growth, and a deeper appreciation for the beauty that abounds when artistry and nature unite as one.

7. The Art of Display: Choosing the Right Stand for Your Bonsai and Pot

In the serene realm of bonsai, where nature and artistry intertwine in a harmonious symphony, the art of display is an essential element that elevates the bonsai experience to new heights. As the stage upon which the living masterpiece takes its place, the stand serves as the foundation for the bonsai tree and pot, uniting them in a tableau of beauty and balance. As we journey through the art of display, let us explore the nuances of choosing the right stand for your bonsai and pot, and uncover the secrets that will elevate your bonsai presentation to a true work of art.

Step 1: Understanding the Role of the Bonsai Stand

In the world of bonsai, the stand is more than just a functional support for the tree and pot; it is an integral part of the overall presentation, enhancing the visual harmony and balance of the display. The right stand can elevate the beauty of your bonsai tree and pot, drawing the viewer's eye to the intricate interplay of form, color, and texture that defines your living artwork.

Step 2: Considering the Style and Size of Your Bonsai and Pot

Before selecting a stand, take a moment to consider the style and size of your bonsai tree and pot. The stand should complement the form and character of the tree, as well as the pot's shape, color, and design. Consider the tree's height, spread, and trunk thickness, as well as the pot's dimensions, to ensure that the stand is appropriately sized and proportioned to support and showcase your bonsai display.

Step 3: Exploring Different Stand Styles and Materials

The world of bonsai stands is rich and diverse, offering a plethora of styles and materials to suit every taste and preference. From traditional Japanese wooden stands with intricately carved designs to sleek, modern metal stands with minimalist lines, the options are endless.

When selecting a stand, consider the overall aesthetic of your bonsai display and choose a style and material that complements and enhances the tree and pot. For example, a traditional Japanese bonsai may be best showcased on a wooden stand with intricate carvings, while a contemporary, abstract bonsai may be better suited to a modern metal or glass stand.

Step 4: Factoring in Display Environment and Conditions

As you choose the perfect stand for your bonsai and pot, consider the environment and conditions in which your display will be showcased. If your bonsai will be displayed outdoors, select a stand made from materials that can withstand the elements, such as stone, metal, or treated wood. For indoor displays, consider the surrounding décor and choose a stand that complements and enhances the aesthetic of the space.

Step 5: Arranging Your Bonsai Display for Maximum Impact

With the ideal stand chosen, it is time to arrange your bonsai display for maximum impact. Place your tree and pot on the stand, ensuring that they are positioned for optimal balance and visual harmony. Consider the viewing angle and adjust the arrangement as needed to showcase the most striking features of your bonsai tree and pot.

Step 6: Caring for Your Bonsai Stand

To preserve the beauty and longevity of your bonsai stand, be sure to care for it properly. Clean the stand regularly to remove dust and debris, and treat the material as needed to maintain its luster and durability. By caring for your stand, you are ensuring that it remains a fitting foundation for your living masterpiece.

In conclusion, the art of display is a vital aspect of the bonsai experience, uniting the tree and pot on a stage that showcases their harmonious interplay of form, color, and texture. By carefully selecting the right stand for your bonsai and pot, and considering factors such as style, size, materials, and display environment, you can create a captivating tableau that elevates your bonsai presentation to new heights. As you journey through the world of bonsai stands, embrace the opportunity to experiment with different styles and materials, and discover the unique combinations that best express your artistic vision.

Step 7: Enhancing Your Bonsai Display with Additional Elements

To further elevate your bonsai display, consider incorporating additional elements such as accent plants, stones, or scrolls. These elements can add depth and context to your presentation, creating a cohesive and visually engaging tableau that tells a story and invites the viewer to explore the world of your bonsai creation.

Step 8: Learning from the Masters of Bonsai Display

As you delve deeper into the art of bonsai display, seek inspiration from the masters of this captivating art form. Study their techniques, arrangements, and philosophies, and apply these lessons to your own bonsai display. By learning from the masters, you can develop a deeper understanding of the principles of balance, harmony, and visual storytelling that define the art of bonsai display.

Step 9: Sharing Your Bonsai Display with the World

With your bonsai display meticulously arranged on the perfect stand, it is time to share your creation with the world. Exhibit your bonsai at local shows, clubs, or online forums, and invite friends and family to enjoy the beauty and serenity of your living artwork. By sharing your bonsai display, you can inspire others to explore the enchanting world of bonsai and contribute to the rich tapestry of artistic expression that defines this timeless art form.

In conclusion, the art of bonsai display is a celebration of the harmonious balance between the tree, pot, and stand, creating a visually captivating tableau that invites the viewer to explore the wonders of nature and human creativity. By selecting the right stand for your bonsai and pot, and carefully arranging your display for maximum impact, you can create a living work of art that inspires, enchants, and captivates the senses. May your journey through the art of display be filled with discovery, inspiration, and a deeper appreciation for the beauty that abounds when artistry and nature unite as one.

8. Caring for Bonsai Pots: Maintenance, Cleaning, and Repairs

In the captivating world of bonsai, where whispers of nature become living art, the bonsai pot plays a crucial role in elevating the tree's beauty to new heights. With the perfect pot in hand, the miniature wonder takes on a new life, harmoniously entwined with its vessel. As we embark on this journey to craft the perfect bonsai pot, let us follow the footsteps that lead us through the art of pottery, creating a masterpiece that will cradle and complement the bonsai's essence.

Step 1: Choosing the Clay

Our journey begins with the selection of clay, the very foundation of our bonsai pot. Choose from the diverse palette of earthenware, stoneware, or porcelain, considering factors such as texture, color, and durability. The clay you select will dictate the pot's final appearance and how it harmonizes with the bonsai tree it will support.

Step 2: Preparing the Clay

Next, we prepare the clay, kneading and wedging it to remove air bubbles and create a consistent, workable texture. This process, though simple, is vital in ensuring the strength and stability of the finished pot, as well as the potter's connection with the earthy material.

Step 3: Shaping the Bonsai Pot

Now, we shape our pot, employing traditional techniques such as hand-building or wheel-throwing, or embracing modern methods like slip-casting or 3D printing. Whichever technique you choose, remember that the pot's shape should complement the bonsai tree's style and form, creating a harmonious balance that allows both elements to shine.

Step 4: Adding Details and Drainage Holes

With the basic form of the pot complete, we turn our attention to the details that will set our bonsai pot apart. Carve, sculpt, or add decorative elements that enhance the pot's character, and don't forget to create drainage holes in the bottom of the pot to ensure the health of the bonsai tree.

Step 5: Drying the Pot

Patience is key in the art of bonsai pottery, as we must now allow our creation to dry slowly and evenly to prevent cracking or warping. This process, known as the bone-dry stage, can take several days or even weeks, depending on the thickness of the pot and the humidity in the environment.

Step 6: Bisque Firing

Once our pot is thoroughly dry, it is time for the first firing, known as bisque firing. Place the pot in a kiln, gradually increasing the temperature to remove any remaining moisture and harden the clay. This process prepares the pot for glazing and helps prevent it from cracking during the final firing.

Step 7: Glazing the Pot

With our bisque-fired pot in hand, we can now explore the world of glazes and finishes. Apply the glaze to your pot, considering the desired color, texture, and finish. Keep in mind that the glaze's hues should complement the bonsai tree's foliage and enhance the pot's overall aesthetic.

Step 8: Glaze Firing

Now, we return our pot to the kiln for the final firing, known as the glaze firing. This process, which often requires higher temperatures than the bisque firing, will transform the applied glaze into a glassy, durable finish that will protect and beautify our bonsai pot for years to come.

Step 9: Admiring Your Creation

With the firing complete, our journey comes to an end, and we can now admire the fruits of our labor. Gaze upon your bonsai pot, a testament to your creativity, skill, and dedication to the art of bonsai pottery. Each curve, detail, and hue reflects the time and care invested in this handcrafted treasure, a vessel worthy of cradling nature's living art.

Step 10: Selecting the Right Bonsai Tree

The perfect bonsai pot deserves the perfect tree. Carefully choose a bonsai tree that complements your pot's shape, color, and style. Consider factors such as the tree's size, form, and growth habits to ensure a harmonious pairing that celebrates both the tree and its vessel.

Step 11: Preparing the Pot and Tree for Planting

Before uniting your bonsai tree with its new home, it is essential to prepare both the pot and tree for planting. Place a layer of mesh over the pot's drainage holes to prevent soil from escaping, and add a layer of well-draining bonsai soil mix to the pot's base. Gently remove the bonsai tree from its current container, teasing out the roots and trimming them as necessary to promote healthy growth.

Step 12: Planting the Bonsai Tree in Your Pot

With your pot and tree prepared, it is time to bring them together as one. Position the bonsai tree in the pot, taking care to arrange the roots evenly and maintain the tree's desired planting angle. Fill the pot with additional bonsai soil, ensuring the roots are completely covered and secure. To settle the soil and remove air pockets, gently tap the pot and water the tree thoroughly.

Step 13: Caring for Your Bonsai Tree and Pot

Now that your bonsai tree and pot are united, it is crucial to provide them with the proper care and attention they need to thrive. Water your bonsai regularly, ensuring the soil remains moist but not waterlogged. Provide the tree with appropriate sunlight, temperature, and humidity for its specific species, and fertilize and prune as necessary to promote healthy growth.

As you care for your bonsai tree and pot, take time to admire the harmonious balance they share. The pot, a product of your creativity and skill, enhances the tree's natural beauty, while the tree brings life and movement to the pot's earthy form. Together, they create a living work of art that celebrates the beauty of nature and the human touch.

In conclusion, the journey to craft the perfect bonsai pot is one of patience, dedication, and artistic expression. As you follow these steps, remember that it is the harmony between the tree and its pot that elevates the bonsai art form to new heights. May your bonsai pot serve as a testament to your love and appreciation for the enchanting world of bonsai, cradling and nurturing nature's whispers as they dance and sway in the gentle embrace of the earth.

9. Bonsai Pots from Around the World: A Cultural Perspective

In the enchanting realm of bonsai, where the whispers of nature take form in living art, the bonsai pot serves as a vessel for the miniature wonder that dances upon its stage. As we journey across the globe, exploring the diverse traditions and cultures that have embraced the art of bonsai pottery, we discover a tapestry of creativity, history, and inspiration that unites us all in our love for these tiny trees and their earthbound homes.

From the Land of the Rising Sun, where the ancient art of bonsai first took root, we encounter the quintessential Japanese bonsai pots. These vessels, crafted with skill and reverence, embody the principles of wabi-sabi, celebrating the beauty of imperfection and the transient nature of life. With their earthy tones, clean lines, and understated elegance, Japanese bonsai pots serve as the foundation for our global exploration of bonsai pottery.

As we sail across the sea to the Middle Kingdom, we find ourselves immersed in the rich history and artistry of Chinese bonsai pots. Known as penjing, the Chinese art of miniature landscapes predates the Japanese bonsai tradition and has its own unique aesthetic. Chinese bonsai pots often feature vibrant colors, intricate patterns, and ornate designs that reflect the country's diverse artistic heritage. These pots, with their distinct character, offer a window into the heart of China's cultural and creative spirit.

Our journey continues to the Korean Peninsula, where the art of bunjae, the Korean counterpart to bonsai, has flourished for centuries. Korean bonsai pots, often crafted from stoneware or porcelain, showcase the nation's rich pottery tradition. With their unique shapes, natural textures, and understated beauty, these pots embody the harmony and balance that define the Korean approach to the art of bonsai.

As we traverse the oceans and continents, we discover the thriving bonsai pot traditions of Europe and the Americas. From the rustic charm of French pots to the innovative designs of modern American artists, these bonsai pots reflect the diverse influences and styles that have shaped the Western world. With their unique blend of old and new, these pots offer a fresh perspective on the art of bonsai pottery, pushing the boundaries of creativity and form.

In the heart of Africa, where the ancient rhythms of the earth pulse through the land, we find bonsai pots that celebrate the continent's vibrant colors, textures, and patterns. African bonsai pots, often crafted from local clay and adorned with traditional motifs, reflect the deep connection between the people and the earth, as well as their love for nature and its endless beauty.

As our journey draws to a close, we find ourselves surrounded by a kaleidoscope of bonsai pots from around the world, each one a testament to the unique traditions, cultures, and artistry that have shaped the global bonsai community. From the earthy simplicity of Japanese pots to the vibrant exuberance of African vessels, these pots remind us that, while the language of bonsai may vary from region to region, the love for these tiny trees and their earthbound homes is universal.

In conclusion, the art of bonsai pottery transcends borders and cultures, uniting us all in our appreciation for the beauty of nature and the human touch. As we gaze upon the bonsai pots from around the world, we are reminded of the rich tapestry of creativity, history, and inspiration that binds us together, and the enduring power of the bonsai art form to connect us all in our shared love for these enchanting miniature wonders.

10. Matching Bonsai Species to Pot Designs: A Comprehensive Guide

In the enchanting world of bonsai, where the whispers of nature are transformed into living art, the delicate dance between tree and pot takes center stage. The harmonious pairing of bonsai species and pot design is a testament to the care, love, and artistry that unites these earthbound wonders. As we delve into the art of matching bonsai species to pot designs, let us explore the beauty, balance, and synergy that emerge from this intricate and captivating relationship.

When selecting the perfect pot for your bonsai tree, the first consideration is the tree's style and form. From the windswept grace of the literati style to the sturdy, grounded presence of the formal upright, each bonsai style has unique characteristics that must be honored and celebrated. The pot's shape and size should complement the tree's form, highlighting its strengths and enhancing its natural beauty.

For formal upright (Chokkan) and informal upright (Moyogi) bonsai styles, choose a pot with a rectangular or oval shape that provides a strong, stable base for the tree. These pots should have clean lines and a balanced design that echoes the tree's structure without overpowering its delicate beauty.

For slanting (Shakan) and windswept (Fukinagashi) styles, consider pots with gentle curves and organic shapes that reflect the dynamic movement of the tree. These pots should have a sense of fluidity and grace, harmoniously mirroring the tree's natural flow and energy.

For cascade (Kengai) and semi-cascade (Han-Kengai) styles, opt for pots with a deeper, more rounded form that can accommodate the tree's dramatic downward growth. These pots should provide ample space for the tree's cascading branches, while maintaining a sense of balance and harmony in the overall composition.

When it comes to the pot's color and finish, consider the hues of the bonsai's foliage and bark, as well as the tree's seasonal changes. Earthy tones, such as browns, grays, and greens, are versatile choices that can complement a wide range of bonsai species. For trees with vibrant foliage, such as the Japanese Maple, consider a pot with a contrasting color that will enhance the tree's natural beauty.

The pot's texture and material should also be taken into account when pairing with a bonsai species. Traditional clay pots, with their natural, organic feel, are well-suited to most bonsai trees, providing a complementary backdrop for the tree's foliage and form. For trees with a more rugged, weathered appearance, such as the Juniper, consider a pot with a rough, textured surface that echoes the tree's rugged beauty.

Finally, when matching a bonsai species to a pot design, consider the cultural and historical context of both the tree and the pot. For traditional Japanese and Chinese bonsai species, such as the Pine or Elm, a pot that reflects the aesthetic and craftsmanship of these ancient cultures will create a harmonious, authentic pairing. For more contemporary or exotic species, such as the tropical Ficus or the Mediterranean Olive, a pot with a modern or unconventional design may provide a refreshing, innovative pairing.

In conclusion, the art of matching bonsai species to pot designs is a delicate balance of form, color, texture, and context. By considering these factors and embracing the unique character of each bonsai tree, we can create a harmonious union between tree and pot, a living masterpiece that celebrates the beauty and synergy of these earthbound wonders. As we explore the endless possibilities of this captivating relationship, let us remember that it is the love, care, and artistry we invest in our bonsai trees and pots that ultimately brings them to life, elevating the whispers of nature into a breathtaking symphony of harmony and balance.

When creating your bonsai masterpiece, take time to observe and understand the tree's individual character, its growth habits, and its unique features. Allow these elements to guide your choice of pot, creating a bespoke partnership that enhances the beauty of both tree and vessel.

As you nurture and care for your bonsai tree, be open to the possibility of change and growth. As the tree matures and evolves, the pot that once provided the perfect home may no longer be the ideal match. Embrace the opportunity to explore new pot designs and styles, finding fresh inspiration and creating a dynamic, ever-evolving partnership between tree and pot.

As you continue on your bonsai journey, be inspired by the creativity and passion of fellow bonsai enthusiasts from around the world. Learn from their experiences, their successes, and their challenges, as you forge your own path in the captivating world of bonsai. Share your knowledge, your insights, and your love for these miniature wonders, as you contribute to the global community of bonsai lovers and help shape the future of this ancient and beloved art form.

In the end, the art of matching bonsai species to pot designs is not just about aesthetics and harmony; it is about the connection between the artist, the tree, and the earth. It is about understanding and embracing the unique character of each bonsai species, and finding a pot that allows that character to shine. By cultivating this deep connection and appreciation for the beauty and balance of the bonsai world, we can create living works of art that inspire, captivate, and enrich our lives, reminding us of the enduring power of nature and the human touch.

11. Inspiring Bonsai Pot Artists: Interviews and Insights from Master Craftsmen

In the enchanting realm of bonsai, where nature's whispers are transformed into living poetry, the bonsai pot serves as both canvas and stage, a testament to the artistry, passion, and creativity that unite these earthbound wonders. As we delve into the world of bonsai pot artists, we invite you to join us on a journey of discovery, where the stories, insights, and inspirations of master craftsmen illuminate the path to our own artistic awakening.

Our voyage begins in the Land of the Rising Sun, where the ancient art of bonsai first took root. Here, we meet master potter Hiroshi Iwata, a living legend whose exquisite pots grace the collections of bonsai enthusiasts around the globe. Through the wisdom of his words and the beauty of his creations, Hiroshi reveals the essence of Japanese bonsai pottery, a delicate balance of form, function, and spirit, guided by the timeless principles of wabi-sabi.

As we journey westward, we encounter the innovative and inspiring work of European potter Peter Krebs, whose fusion of traditional and contemporary techniques has earned him a place among the bonsai world's most respected craftsmen. In our intimate interview, Peter shares his insights into the creative process, the challenges and rewards of his craft, and the endless possibilities that emerge when we embrace our artistic calling with courage, curiosity, and passion.

Across the ocean, in the heart of the American bonsai community, we meet the remarkable Sara Rayner, whose distinctive pots have captured the hearts and imaginations of collectors and enthusiasts alike. As Sara shares her journey from aspiring artist to renowned potter, we discover the power of perseverance, the joy of self-discovery, and the transformative beauty that blooms when we nurture our dreams and follow our hearts.

In the sun-drenched landscapes of the Mediterranean, we encounter the visionary potter, Lorenzo Banchi, whose striking pots embody the vibrant colors, textures, and patterns of his beloved homeland. Through our conversation with Lorenzo, we delve into the cultural influences that shape his work, the artistic heritage that inspires him, and the boundless creative spirit that drives him to push the boundaries of bonsai pottery and redefine the art form itself.

As we travel the world, exploring the stories and inspirations of these master craftsmen, we are reminded that the art of bonsai pottery is not just about creating beautiful vessels for our beloved trees; it is about the human connection, the shared passion, and the universal language of creativity that unites us all. Through their words and their work, these master potters offer us a glimpse into the heart and soul of the bonsai community, a vibrant tapestry of art, culture, and inspiration that spans the globe and transcends time.

In conclusion, the inspiring stories and insights of these master bonsai pot artists serve as a beacon of light for our own artistic journeys, guiding us towards a deeper understanding of the art form and a greater appreciation for the beauty and balance that define the world of bonsai. As we embark on our own creative explorations, let us carry their wisdom in our hearts and their passion in our hands, and may the enchanting dance between tree and pot continue to inspire, captivate, and nourish our souls for generations to come.

12. The Future of Bonsai Pottery: Innovations and Emerging Trends

In the magical world of bonsai, where nature's whispers are woven into living masterpieces, the bonsai pot serves as a vessel for the dreams and aspirations of artists and enthusiasts alike. As we gaze into the future of bonsai pottery, we embark on a journey of discovery and innovation, where emerging trends and cutting-edge technologies pave the way for a new era of creativity, connection, and collaboration in the enchanting realm of these miniature wonders.

As we peer into the horizon, we find ourselves captivated by the evolving role of technology in the world of bonsai pottery. From 3D printing and digital design tools to advanced materials and fabrication techniques, the future of bonsai pot creation promises to be a vibrant fusion of art and science, where the boundaries of imagination are expanded and the possibilities for innovation are endless.

In the realm of materials, we see the emergence of eco-friendly and sustainable alternatives to traditional clay and ceramic pots. From biodegradable plant-based resins to reclaimed and recycled materials, these innovative solutions offer a glimpse into a future where the beauty of bonsai is in harmony with the health and wellbeing of our planet.

As we explore the future of bonsai pot design, we encounter a world where the marriage of form and function reaches new heights of sophistication and elegance. From modular and adjustable pots that adapt to the changing needs of the tree to self-watering and nutrient-delivery systems that enhance the health and vitality of the bonsai, these innovations herald a new age of convenience, versatility, and performance in the art of bonsai pottery.

In the ever-changing landscape of global culture, we witness the emergence of new aesthetic trends and styles that reflect the diverse influences and inspirations of the bonsai community. From the bold, minimalist designs of Scandinavian pottery to the vibrant colors and patterns of Latin American ceramics, these emerging trends offer a fresh perspective on the art of bonsai pottery, challenging our assumptions and expanding our horizons.

As the bonsai world becomes increasingly interconnected through digital platforms and social media, we see the rise of a new generation of artists and enthusiasts who collaborate, share, and learn from one another, transcending geographical and cultural boundaries. This global community fosters a spirit of innovation and experimentation, where the exchange of ideas and techniques fuels the evolution of bonsai pottery and the continued growth of the art form.

In conclusion, the future of bonsai pottery promises to be an exhilarating journey of discovery, innovation, and collaboration, where the whispers of nature are brought to life through the skill, passion, and creativity of artists and enthusiasts around the world. As we embrace the emerging trends and technologies that shape this evolving landscape, let us remember that the true essence of bonsai pottery lies not in the materials, tools, or techniques we use, but in the love, care, and artistry we invest in our tiny trees and their earthbound homes. For it is through this devotion that we create living masterpieces that inspire, captivate, and nourish our souls, reminding us of the enduring beauty and wonder of the bonsai art form.